Horn of Plenty –
The Cornucopia of Your Life

by

Blythe Ayne, Ph.D.

Books & Audio by Blythe Ayne, Ph.D.

Nonfiction:
Love Is The Answer
45 Ways To Excellent Life
Life Flows on the River of Love
Finding Your Path, Engaging Your Purpose
Horn of Plenty—The Cornucopia of Your Life
Write Your Book! Publish Your Book! Market Your Book!

How to Save Your Life Series:
Save Your Life With The Power Of pH Balance
Save Your Life With The Phenomenal Lemon
Save Your Life with Stupendous Spices
Save Your Life with the Elixir of Water

Fiction:
The Darling Undesirables Series:
The Heart of Leo - short story prequel
The Darling Undesirables
Moons Rising
The Inventor's Clone
Hearts Quest

Short Story Collections:
5 Minute Stories
Lovely Frights for Lonely Nights

Children's Illustrated Books:
The Rat Who Didn't Like Rats
The Rat Who Didn't Like Christmas

Poetry:
Home & the Surrounding Territory

CD:
The Power of pH Balance –
Dr. Blythe Ayne Interviews Steven Acuff

Horn of Plenty –
The Cornucopia of Your Life

by

Blythe Ayne, Ph.D.

Horn of Plenty–The Cornucopia of Your Life
Blythe Ayne, Ph.D.

Emerson & Tilman, Publishers
129 Pendleton Way #55
Washougal, WA 98671

www.HornOfPlenty.BlytheAyne.com

All Rights Reserved
No part of this publication may be reproduced, distributed, or transmitted
in any form, or by any means, including photocopying, recording,
or other electronic or mechanical methods, without the prior
written permission of the author, except brief quotations
in critical reviews and other noncommercial
uses permitted by copyright law.

All graphics & text © Blythe Ayne, Ph.D.
www.BlytheAyne.com

Horn of Plenty–The Cornucopia of Your Life
ISBN: 978-0-9827835-7-3

[1. BODY, MIND & SPIRIT/General
2. BODY, MIND & SPIRIT/Inspiration
3. BODY, MIND & SPIRIT/Mindfulness & Meditation] I. Title
BIC: FM

First Edition

DEDICATION:
*To all who desire to receive
And to share
Life's Amazing Riches*

Horn of Plenty –
The Cornucopia of Your Life

Table of Contents

Chapter One – You Are At Cause	*1*
Chapter Two – Unite Your Heart & Your Mind	*11*
Chapter Three – Thought In Three Dimensions	*17*
Chapter Four – Being A Conscious Being	*27*
Chapter Five – Divine Mind Is At Cause	*33*
Chapter Six – Needs Met – Desires Fulfilled	*41*
Chapter Seven – Your Unique Light	*49*
Chapter Eight – Your Source Cares For You	*55*
Chapter Nine – Becoming Fulfilled	*61*
Chapter Ten – Love — Gratitude — Abundance	*67*
My Gift for You	*74*
About the Author	*75*

Be

Love

Image & Text © Blythe Ayne

Chapter One

You Are At Cause

When you turn your focus on the source, that is to say, what is at *cause* in your life, you'll then be able to enjoy the *effects*. This cause-effect relationship is how the Universe operates.

*Understanding what is at **Cause**
And what is at **Effect**
Is how the flow of plenty
Is determined in your life.*

Let us imagine this source, this creative force, as the horn of plenty, from which all good things flow. This endless flow of powerful manifestation is the same energy that keeps planets in orbit around the sun, and is the same energy—the same source—that beats your heart and breathes your lungs. The creative force is also individualized as you.

> *"Life goes on within you
> and without you."*
> *The Beatles*

There is an omnipresent being-ness—creative force, universal intelligence, web of knowing—which is, at its core, what we might look upon as infinitely generous.

Attached to this primary and important premise of infinite generosity is its partner, receiving. There can be no giving without receiving.
One hand shakes another.

Electricity and magnets must have a positive and a negative charged pole.

The circuit of giving is fulfilled in receipt.

It's good to practice generously receiving all that life offers us—whether gifts from people, the wonders of nature, or simply appreciating the miracle of breath.

As a therapist, and, indeed, as a student of life, I've encountered many people who are not capable of receiving. They may be blocked by guilt, or a false sense of responsibility, or a belief that they are not worthy, or a determination not to be beholding to anyone—any or all of these reasons, and more.

Have you ever met a person unwilling to happily accept gifts from you, or others, or life?

Does this, perhaps, describe you?

Give serious consideration to shifting your beliefs. Open up to receiving all the gifts of life, whether a humble item from someone, or a glorious sunset. Be present at the horn of plenty, and be filled with gratitude for all that tumbles out of it into your life.

Creations Inspire Creating

Have you ever thought about how, in just this little sliver of the visible universe where we live and that we can witness, there is an inexhaustible "plethora of plenty"—life-forms, stars, planets, love, beauty, water, air, earth, fabulous creatures, "mind-stuff"—so forth and so on, and so on and so forth? How stunning, exciting and beguiling the creative force is!

What is the invitation of all of this plethora of creative energy? Are you not being called, too, to *create, create, create?*

Why staunch this flow with any thought of lack, poverty, need? We far too often slip into the hypnotic and terrible habit of believing there is not enough. Of thinking we need more.

This hypnotic thought process is the reason for poverty and for the ridiculous trillions of dollars of ever-climbing debt around the world.

Only by becoming very consciously aware of thoughts and language and actions that affirm lack—consciously, attentively, changing these habits—will we begin to change both our individual lives, and the life of our planet.

We inhabit a plentiful universe. There is enough for every person to live a beautiful and fulfilling life.

What if we stopped focusing our creative powers on denying abundant flow? What if, instead, we focused our amazing creative powers upon affirming abundant flow?

A concrete example will help us look at this concept. Let's consider money. We invented money.

The purpose of money is to be used as a symbol of value of exchange in order to make bartering easier.

If I want your orange, but you don't want my apple, I can give you something else that you can use, like ... money!

If money is a concept whose only purpose is to streamline the exchange of goods and services, why give it a power of its own? It's nothing other than a concept. It's purpose is to make it easier for us to interact, and therefore, easier to get along.

Why empower the illusion of money with the illusion of lack?

Affirm Your Plentiful Life

Your "you-ness" is so amazing! Your existence is proof of profound abundance. You have a limitless ability to create continually, pouring from the center of your being where your creative forces reside.

The creative force has created all that is. So, continuing to manifest in your life is only logical. Again, don't focus on the idea of lack. Be filled with gratitude for the plenty that surrounds you. You call to you what you focus on.

If you're tired of feeling like you do not have enough, *TURN AROUND!* Change how you look at things. As Dr. Wayne Dyer said, "When you change the way you look at things, the things you look at change."

Four Ways to Initiate the Flow of Plenty

There are innumerable ways to stimulate the flow of plenty, but let us lay a ground-work, a place to start, by considering these four:

1. Acknowledge, name, and contemplate the many small miracles that occur every day in your life.

Every day is an endless series of miracles: seeing, hearing, tasting, touching, the scent of flowers, or fresh air, or hot tea ... *oh!* The list goes on, and on, and on.

2. Be filled with gratitude for all the blessings you can name.

And be filled with gratitude for no particular reason at all.

3. List actions you can take to nurture your acknowledgment of the plentiful blessings you experience.

Drop everything. Listen to a bird sing, watch a sunset, really see the shadows in the evening playing on the wall, listen to—and truly hear—a child's guileless giggle.

You cannot buy any of these things if you had a trillion-trillion dollars. The most amazing reasons for being alive are enjoyed by your five senses.

AWAKEN! Appreciate the endless gifts of life. This is so far superior to the hypnotized, frustrated, sleepwalking state that many people are in much of the time.

4. Shift your inner picture away from *lack* to *plenty*. Why not start right now? Visualize your own cornucopia pouring out everything, everything, necessary for you to sustain a beautiful life.

Enjoying Your Plentiful Life

If everywhere around you, you see the abundance of a creative, plentiful universe, why wouldn't it be the same for you? Ultimately, everything comes together for good.

You are a powerful being! You are prosperous simply because you breathe. The breath of life has been bestowed upon you—make the most of it. Believe in yourself.

We've been created in the image of our Creator. Thus, we are creative too. It's the motivation for existence—to create in the way your particular gifts reveal themselves.

What do you desire to create? A work of art, a garden, a child? Be filled with the pleasure of creation and create with excitement and joy. Allow your life to be filled with the myriad options of plenty, tap into the all-pervasive, powerful, creative, manifesting energy. Love every minute and every nuance of your life.

Scarcity in any form such as poverty, prejudice, paucity, corruption, depravity, hostility, greed, guilt, selfishness, negative self-esteem, self-hate, hate of others, so forth and so on—have nothing to do with the positive power of creative force. It is time (and long past time) that we set those negatives aside.

All forms of lack are un-whole, unwholesome and unholy. Anyone who says or feels life is not plentiful has moved away from the source of plenty.

All things are whole
In the mind of the Creator

Points for Contemplation & Action:

- I am learning what is at Cause, and what is at Effect in my life.

- Giving is receiving—I am generous with both.

- The Creative Force ceaselessly creates, and is my role model.

- I will never lose sight of the miracle embodied as *ME*.

- I keep my focus on what I desire to manifest—because what I focus on manifests.

- I am filled with gratitude for the wonderful abundance in my life.

- Money is a symbol of plenty—not a symbol of poverty.

- I have been created to create!

> *"Expect your every need to be met.*
> *Expect the answer to every problem,*
> *Expect abundance on every level..."*
> *Eileen Caddy*

Heart-Mind In Balance

From: Horn of Plenty © Blythe Ayne

Chapter Two

Unite Your Heart & Your Mind

What does it mean to have a united Heart-Mind? In our contemporary world, there is an emphasis on intelligence, and a considerable value placed on great thinkers. All well and good, however, you cannot get very far if your heart is not in alignment with your mind.

The endeavors of the greatest thinkers have always been in alignment with their heart. That is to say, their feelings interweave with their thinking. Commitment is a measure of emotional engagement.

Have you ever known someone who had an average talent, but a burning passion regarding their talent?

Maybe you were surprised one day to discover that this person has become quite successful in pursuing that passion.

And yet, on another hand, have you ever known a person with a notable genius, but year in and year out, never becoming successful in the field of their obvious raw genius?

The difference between these two people comes from the extent to which each one burns with an unrelenting passion for their calling, and the extent to which they connect their feelings for their calling with the work they invest in it.

In other words, they have a united Heart-Mind. When your heart is yoked to your mind, your endeavors grow wings and take off.

Manifesting Plenty in Your World

The heart feels, the mind thinks. Each has its power. Feeling and thinking, when on the same wavelength, become united in:
- Intention
- Desire
- Understanding
- Focus
- Manifestation

Keep your focus on your intentions. Keep out compromising, intrusive, scattering, negative emotions and thoughts. Staying focused on your aspirations is the heart of prosperity.

Prosperity isn't only possessions or monetary wealth. The greatest wealth is happiness, contentment, joy, peace, satisfaction.

Creativity and prosperity are on the same path. When you attend to your creativity, prosperity is right there. Release niggling distractions. Lay claim to your prosperity in the name of higher energies and in the realm of unconditional love.

Discard the parts of your Id and Ego that run irrelevant, chatty scenarios and unsettling, immaterial fears.

Fear writes dark messages on the blank page of the future. Instead, write positive messages of fulfillment, joy, and love in your diary of the future.

Raise your consciousness and hone and nurture your intelligence. Be lovingly attentive to your heart—the hub of your emotions. This is how you unite your thinking to your feeling processes. Intentional moderation of mind and heart will bring you to the throne of your own, internal, Divine Presence.

The "I AM" of the Creator is the "I AM" in you, and from that source, you engage in the wealth of your experience.

Become familiar with the many energies flowing about you that will assist you in your purpose, and ask higher energies to prevail in your life.

Whatever you desire, affirm that it's on its way, then release the thought.

Again, your calling is the WHAT. The HOW is coming to you on the interconnected web of existence.

Let's consider this metaphor. Let's say you've decided to take a cruise from Seattle to Alaska. The WHAT is, "taking a cruise," the HOW is the route the ship will take to get you there. You bask in the pleasure of the WHAT beforehand in excited anticipation, during your vacation when the event expands in your reality, and afterwards in fond and intriguing memories.

You entrusted the ship's captain to take care of HOW you got there. I'm suggesting that you let your own "ship's captain"—that is to say, your higher self, and the energies of the *web of being*—to do the same regarding HOW your life's work, your heart's desires, will arrive.

Clear information will be revealed as you move on your journey. Just as for your vacation you were given instructions to be at a certain location at a certain time to embark on your journey, the same will prove true regarding your life's work.

Points for Contemplation & Action:

- I unite my Heart with my Mind, and my feelings with my thoughts. This is the "alchemy" of manifestation.

- Clear intentions and focus will clarify for me my purpose.

- What I desire is on its way. I don't need to know how, I simply need to know that this is true. I affirm that I will keep the future open and positive by being thoroughly engaged in the moment, and thinking, feeling, and doing that which is in alignment with my intentions.

- I ask my angels—or any energy or power that I believe angels to be—to assist me with my purpose.

> *"When you are grateful,*
> *fear disappears and*
> *abundance appears."*
> **Anthony Robbins**

Chapter Three

Thought Arising In The Three Dimensions

Your unique genius, the creator living in you, is as prosperous as the creative force everywhere else. This infinite, ever-flowing creative process is continually filtering through many dimensions to the seemingly solid three-dimensions.

Thought becomes manifest. The purer the thought, the clearer the manifestation. That is to say, the more "together" a thought, the more rapidly it manifests in concrete form.

To say again what I've said before, wealth is not the point of manifesting anything. Happiness is the objective. Inspiration, joy, creativity, sharing, loving and peace are the true objectives of existence.

Would you agree?

People pursue money for those objectives, not for money itself. People who appear to be pursuing money for money's sake have some wires crossed.

Having known in my life several billionaires, the ones who pursue money for money itself admit to their unhappiness. I believe this is because they don't know *WHY* they are pursuing money. However, the purpose of money remains to nurture love, inspiration, creativity, joy, peace.

Thinking that money, itself, causes deep and lasting happiness removes one's thoughts and feelings away from its reason for being. Everyone desires to be safe and to be happy. Become clear on your motivaition to be safe and happy, and what it takes to find yourself safe and happy will be yours.

Money has upon it the energy of all the wishes and desires of everyone, and therefore is not a clean, clear message to your creating consciousness, nor to your energy field. Nor is it a clear message to the creative forces of the universe.

Constant Activity of Creative Mind

If you have now become aware of the constant activity of Creative Mind, functioning with every breath you breathe, consider the advantage in aligning all your thoughts and feelings with these creative forces.

Become consciously engaged in the unceasing activity of Creative Mind, lay claim every moment to the light of your truth. Creative Mind is lavish, generous, and constructive.

Although, in truth, there's no such thing as generous. The definition of generous is: showing kindness toward others. But if all is *ONE* then excellent care of another is excellent care of yourself. That's simply being active in the creation of more light.

At the Speed of Light

Consciously or unconsciously, your mind creates faster than you can bring the plethora of creations into physical form. Focus on bringing your profuse creativity into the light, where truth and prosperity prevail.

That which assists you while you are creative, loving, kind, prosperous, and doing deeds anonymously, is also good for everyone. You are a power station—

energy flows through you. Like any power station, once energy flows in, it must flow out.

Within you there is a constant activity of creation and prosperity. In order to call your fondest hopes and wishes into reality, behave as if both your being and the actions of your heart's desire are flowing into the three dimensions this very moment.

> *Live in a way that if*
> *everyone lived as you do,*
> *the ills of the planet would be healed.*
> **Blythe Ayne, Ph.D.**

Your Light

You are filled with the light of:
Love
Creation
Prosperity

We've made up the picture of "lack" because we've gotten an idea that having more than others makes us "better." And if we're better than others, then surely we must be happier.

For this picture to work, there has to be people who are worse off than ourselves, and who are, therefore, unhappy.

For anyone capable of thinking, it's an unacceptable premise to desire anyone to be unhappy.

Somewhere in the past, lost in the mists of time, humanity agreed to the hierarchy supporting the illusion, "I am better than you." But we don't need this hierarchy—we only need each and every person fully engaged with their talents, inspiration, enthusiasm and joy, each in a unique and precious way. Imagining. Creating. Manifesting.

Let me emphasize that the creative presence inside you is the source of your affluence.

This presence is constantly creating and bringing into your reality that which you focus and dwell upon. So, be sure that what you focus and dwell upon is what you mean to manifest.

Clarify your thoughts. Remove the cobwebs of negative thoughts and replace them with a bright and clear positive, simple, repetitive statement.

Call it what you will—affirmation, mantra, or just simply, "my happy thought," such as:

> "I choose to be happy."
> *Wayne Dyer*

> "All things are working together perfectly
> for the good of all."
> *Louise Hay*

> "All things are whole in the mind of the Creator."
> *Mary Baker Eddy*

The ever-obedient force responds—and can only respond—to the immutable laws of the universe. In this case, the creative force manifests what you repeat—what you command—with your affirmation or mantra.

What you pictured in thought, supported by your emotion, will return in form. These are the building blocks of the three dimensions.

You are making choices. You can choose to be opulently comfortable or opulently poverty-stricken. It remains an opulent universe in either case. Trust and know that you call your life lessons to you.

Excellent Choices

When you feel you've learned enough about abuse, victimization, poverty, pain, sadness, anger, hurt, depravation, loneliness, fear, frustration, guilt, so on and so forth, you'll begin to consciously make different choices.

And when that happens, you'll have empathy for the lives people live, and how their choices influence the outcomes they experience. You'll become tolerant, feeling unconditional love toward them, seeing that they, like you, are simply learning the lessons they are calling to themselves.

The only difference is that perhaps they don't yet realize their own influence on the events of their lives. You, on the other hand, are further along the path having understood this truth. Be mindful that your light sheds light upon the path for others.

There is no place for prejudice, there in only a call to *LOVE UNCONDITIONALLY*.

Choose Wisdom

Sometimes it's difficult to see the results of our weak and unwise thoughts and feelings, leading to weak and unwise choices. Perhaps we have to see the shadow cast by less-than-ideal or even self-destructive choices in others before we have an understanding about the significance of making wiser choices ourselves.

But consider the advance you'll make in your own life, your own manifestations, if you now, this moment, make a pledge to take full responsibility for your thoughts and feelings, monitoring them lovingly. Pledge to have a clearing thought when negativity, self-doubt, and judgmental thoughts and feelings interlope in the terrain of your creative truths.

Points for contemplation and action:

- Happiness and peace are the objectives of manifesting, not money or things.

- I call my life lessons to myself. Why not have them happy and pleasant experiences, rather than from the school of hard knocks?

- I practice unrelenting, unconditional love. I keep the circuit of my Power Station open and flowing.

- Wisdom requests that I remain centered on unconditional love.

- I lovingly monitor my thoughts and feelings. I Immediately replace negativity with a clearing, positive, thought.

> *"Life in abundance
> comes only through great love."*
> **Elbert Hubbard**

Chapter Four

Being A Conscious Being

We've been shown by exemplary lives such as Mother Theresa, Christ, the Buddha and others, what it is to live as a CONSCIOUS BEING. Your own Conscious Being is your personal aspect of the infinite, omniscient, creative force.

Be a Conscious Being! Be mindful, live mindfully.

Draw your Conscious Being into your connected thinking and into your emotionally aware Heart-Mind. Buddhists refer to this as *bodhichitta*, a potent power connection.

A power station has power flowing into and out of it, constantly.

Your Heart-Mind power connection is considerably more powerful than that power station. You are a source of power, with energy flowing in and out, receiving and giving, constantly. Nothing can stop this energy flowing through you—except your will.

Many people engage their will to stop up their energy, creating unfulfilled lives of disarray, guilt, pain, disappointment and unhappiness. It's strangely counterintuitive behavior—while equally strangely common.

The Creative Force, that uniting energy behind the scenes, is your power supply. Your mind ceaselessly imagines, intuits, and is spontaneously aware of new ideas, insights, creations, inventions, and *aha's!*, as well as spiritual knowing, and wisdom.

Your Divine Self attracts that which is similar to it—abundance, equanimity, creativity, happiness, exuberance, and anticipatory excitement about what's unfolding. The "attracting" has already occurred.

Open the door with the sign that reads: *"BELIEF"* and let what you've attracted come in, if you haven't done this already.

Picture Creativity

Picture your creativity. Daily meditate upon an affirmation that states you will be cared for in every way; physically, mentally, spiritually. Entrust your well-being to the energies and sources that attend perfectly to it.

Your source of love is also your source of creative ability, your Horn of Plenty. Creative ability is an aspect of love. Love is the "Being" and creating is the "Doing" of your personal trinity of Creator–Awareness–Self.

Draw into your heart more love than you can hold. This love will continually overflow and pour into other hearts, stopping up worthless thoughts and painful feelings, as they shrink into nothing in the presence of ever-expanding love.

The Creator Within

When you become aware of the creator within you, you will call upon this boundless creative and unconditionally loving source to expand your own unconditional love, and by this process you'll bring positive, meaningful events into the reality of your life.

In such an environment of love—self-love, metta, unconditional love of all of life, in all its forms—you'll be able to do your work without distraction.

Claim this affirmation:

"I am prosperous, able to create every day
for my peace and contentment,
and for the betterment of all,
in all dimensions inside and outside of time."

Points for contemplation and action:

- My Divine Self inspires my creative expressions.

- I am becoming a fully Conscious Being.

- I have been created to create.

- I am a "magnet" of unconditional love, I allow it to fill me up and overflow onto others.

> *"Whatever we are waiting for —*
> *peace of mind, contentment, grace,*
> *the inner awareness of simple*
> *abundance –it will surely come to us,*
> *but only when we are ready to receive it*
> *with an open and grateful heart."*
> **Sarah Ban Breathnach**

Chapter Five

Divine Mind Is At Cause

No person, place or thing is at cause in your life. These are the effects of your focus.

If you try to place any person, place, or thing "at cause" in your feeling-thinking, Heart-Mind, your power connection is corrupted. The illusion of any person, place or thing at cause will interfere with your goals, your life's work and your heart's desires.

Your Heart-Mind awareness of the all-providing nature of Divine Mind, both within you and external to you, is centering and empowering.

The more you become aware that it is your own Heart-Mind at your center, and that it is your base of power, the more it's free to manifest as prosperity in physical form, in addition to spiritual, psychological, emotional and intellectual forms.

> *Divine Mind is at **cause**,*
> *Our senses enjoy this as **effects***

These effects include the wide-range of life experiences such as beautiful sunsets, feelings of love, inspiring philosophical concepts, and so forth. The all-providing nature of Divine Mind is unlimited, and divine effects are also unlimited.

Really, Truly Living

The phrase "making a living" has nothing to do with money, because making a living is another way of saying "making a life," and money is not making a life. It's merely the WD-40 we squirt on our squeaky hinges. It's not the hinge itself.

So, there exists a completely upside-down idea that "making a living" is about money. Many, many, people have lives completely focused on getting a thing that is not the purpose of life.

Money itself is not a livelihood. Livelihood comes from the ability to create from your center. Provision comes from Divine Mind, and as your understanding of this limitless source expands, what you manifest also expands.

It's a choice you make.

This manifestation becomes ever more immediate as your energy shifts into creative empowerment and self-realization. If you have a need, it becomes fulfilled, if you have a desire, it becomes fulfilled.

Thinking From the End

Visualize the result you desire. Then work backwards from that point to NOW, with a clear picture of what you must think, feel, and do, to bring each step into reality, until you arrive at the present moment.

Write down each step, starting at the bottom of a page and working to the top.

Then take each visualized step from the top (which is this moment), and work your way to your desired goal. You will move through conscious mind and feeling body, creating and manifesting.

If you hit a wall with any step and can't seem to accomplish it, ask yourself, "how to do I break this step down into smaller steps?"

Then write those baby steps out in a mini "thinking from the end." In this way, no matter how small the step, there is always forward motion.

Eventually, the present moment and your goal come together.

PRESENT MOMENT >>> <<< FUTURE GOAL

Your Supply

Your supply—and by supply I mean the inspiration, the resources, the understanding, the higher energies, in other words, all the "materials" whether physical or conceptual—is not money, people, places, or things.

The source of your joy, contentment, and centered, balanced, living comes from your Divine Mind.

As mentioned previously, and can never be too-often contemplated, receiving is giving, and giving is receiving. Stay in gratitude to experience and to express unconditional love.

Money Does Not Make the World Go 'Round

Money is not your Being. The human family contrived money as a convenience, a shorthand, of communication so that we could:

1. Get on with the business of *BEING*, and of appreciating the beauty and wonders that surround us.

2. Have more time to focus on unconditional love for ourselves and others.

3. Freely engage in our own creative process.

Move yourself away from the addiction of "having." Humanity has largely gotten itself in to a loop of thinking we need everything we see, rather than simply have appreciation for things we do not need. This is how money moved from being a convenience, to something pursued as if it has a life of its own.

The servant has become the master.

Points for contemplation and action:

• My livelihood comes from the ability to create from my center.

• The more I understand that my provision comes from the limitless expansion of Divine Mind, the more limitless and expansive my manifestations become.

• I practice thinking from the end. I visualize the desired result, then work backwards, writing each step down that I need to do to get to my goal. Then I take action.

• Divine Mind—not people, places, or things—is my supply. I go to the appropriate warehouse to get my life supplies. There are only first rate materials at Divine Mind.

• I live within gratitude, I express unconditional love.

> *"Riches are not from abundance of worldly goods, but from a contented mind."*
> **Anonymous**

Chapter Six

All Your Needs Met – All Your Desires Fulfilled

Your interior, personal, divine self perpetually manifests according not only to your needs, but also your desires. This is the energy of plenitude in action.

Affirm that you have no needs unmet and no desires unfulfilled. Believe that anything that is not presently manifested in you life is on its way. You don't need to have troubling or negative thoughts regarding it.

If you are manifesting what you need as you need it, you have no need.

The focus of your intention and the manifesting of your heart's desires flow into the three-dimensions continuously.

If your focus and intention are directed at the highest and best for all, your manifestations can only have the effect of making you and others happy, peaceful, and fulfilled.

Your desires and wishes are constantly becoming formed. Believe you are provided for so you can attend to your highest calling without lower distractions. In other words, supply responds to demand. Make sure your demands are congruent with your intentions.

Life is But a Dream

This life is a dream. If you choose to awaken from this dream, just as in a lucid dream you can determine how events transpire, you can determine how events transpire in this Dream of Life, constrained only by your wobbling in and out of an aware and awakened state, or by trying to control it rather than letting it flow.

This can be a tricky notion. Jack Canfield, and others who are successful at manifesting and who understand flow in their own lives, explains it in this way that I have already discussed: you don't get caught up in the "how," you keep yourself focused on the "what," and leave the "how" up to your higher power, or the Creative Force, or God, or however you see the continuum.

Relinquish attempting to control, and continue to move forward, attending to the business of your intentions.

Being in Flow

Here's a personal story of being in flow. Recently, I had to buy tires. I was aware that day of being in a particularly calm and transcendent state.

When I got to the tire store, the employee who helped me was quite ill. When I commented that he appeared not well, he told me he had strep throat. I wrote down "Zicam and Oscillococcinum" on a piece of paper and handed it to him.

"Get these," I said, "they will keep you from getting this sick again."

I then was given used-but-like-new radial tires, had my alignment checked and tires balanced ... all free of charge in response to my heartfelt concern for the employee. (In addition, unbeknownst to him, I "prayed him well" as I waited for the work on my vehicle to be completed.)

It took longer to do this work than I'd anticipated. I had a 3:30 acupuncture appointment which was fast approaching, with a considerable distance to drive across town. But I affirmed that I would walk through my acupuncturist's office door at 3:30.

When I walked through the door and looked at the clock, it was *EXACTLY* 3:30! This was a virtual impossibility in the so-called real world, as I left the tire store at 3:20 and it was, at the very minimum, a half-hour drive across town. But in the flow and manifesting world, anything is possible.

Practice Relinquishing

You cannot force flow.

But you can feel when you're in flow, when you're in a place where you've relinquished anxiety, fear, worry, frustration, and attempts to control.

One of the best ways to know when you're not in flow is to listen to your own language.

If you hear yourself using the word "control" ("I can't control my children," "I'm trying to control my employees," etc.), or control-like language ("I'll make him do it," "they had better obey me," "I forced the issue," "how can I compel you to agree?" "I must keep my emotions in check," etc., etc.), you can know that you're distancing yourself from flow.

Have you ever noticed that the more you attempt to exert control, the more things go haywire?

Your Source reveals and manifests form according to your desires and your needs. When you have a clear understanding of this, you are hooking up to an immutable law of the Universe.

There are unlimited, omnipresent, omnipotent resources available to you. You can manifest according to your needs and desires, especially when your desires are related to your calling. As your Divine Self is the source of all sources, all you need do is picture an outcome, and it is done—there's no need to struggle.

Struggle is a road block you throw in your path when you have energy and beliefs around not being able to have things, or beliefs about not being able to be at peace without struggle.

Yes, the Law of Attraction Works

As you come to understand, and to know from experience, that the Law of Attraction absolutely works, absolutely brings to you what you are calling to you, you'll release the struggle, and continue to release it.

If your circumstances are not what you desire, search inside yourself to discover how you called these circumstances to you. Then change your beliefs, change your actions.

Negate the Negative

If you say, "I don't want to be sick, I don't want to be sick," you are calling sickness to you, plain and simple. Instead, call excellent health to yourself. "I love it when I'm perfectly healthy." "I feel *GREAT* today!"

The subconscious does not understand negatives, so when you think or say, "I don't want to be sick," it hears, "I want to be sick." And, often, you will become sick. If you say, "I don't want to be late," the subconscious hears, "I want to be late," and the probability is high that you will be late.

Become aware of this unintentional claim to the negative everywhere in your personal affirmations. Change your language, whether verbalized or silent thoughts, into positives.

Earth Energies

Be aware of the earth energies all around you, surrounding you. They are longing to manifest. Have an invocation that all earth energies manifest for the good of all, without harm or stress to any person, place, or thing, anywhere, in any dimension, throughout time.

Request that the earth energies purely manifest, without you having to put your mind to it. You need your mind to concentrate on, and to manifest, your own creations, insights, and wisdom.

Points for contemplation and action:

- I manifest what I need, as I need it, therefore, I have no need.

- By being awake and in flow with Life, I powerfully manifest.

- When my desires are related to my life's purpose, there are unlimited omnipresent resources available to me.

- The Law of Attraction will answer my call and bring to me what I focus on.

- I invoke earth energies to manifest the highest and best for all.

- I transform all negative language into positive language, to send a clear message to that which manifests.

> *"I keep the telephone of my mind open to peace, harmony, health, love and abundance.*
>
> *Then whenever doubt, anxiety, or fear try to call me, they keep getting a busy signal — soon they'll forget my number."*
> **Edith Armstrong**

Chapter Seven

Your Unique Light

Divine Consciousness continually creates and brings into being everything you require. Accept and understand this truth.

Let go and let the creative force—augmenting through you—become the prism of all the inspiration, healing, and opulence that your particular prism can produce.

The laser pure light of the creative force moves through you, and by this means, you create more light.

Divine Consciousness always takes care of you, but ideas of being unprotected can get in the way.

Believing you are safe and cared for will free you to be at cause and to create. The result of *creating at cause* is *abundance at effect*.

Keep your attention at cause. Continue to create, and the desired effects will follow.

Cause then Effect — an Immutable Law Of the Seen and Unseen Universe

The cornucopia of Divine Consciousness ceaselessly pours out everything you need. Keep your focus on this truth and everything else falls into place.

The Creative Force created you. The Creative Force also creates *for* you—if this were not true, we wouldn't be here.

Your Divine Nature is to be creative. Relinquish distracting, disempowering thoughts. Be in a state of calm. Winds may blow and even knock down trees, but you are safe in the house built by the Creator, which is your body-mind-soul.

This recently happened to me, literally. A gigantic, tree-sized, fifteen foot branch on the tree outside my bedroom window broke off in a terrible windstorm during the night.

I could see where it had broken off the tree—it had been facing perpendicular to the house, pointing at the window. It had no place to go but through the window (and also my computer) and ought to have torn siding off the house as it came down.

But it had, somehow, moved ninety degrees and fell perfectly parallel to the house, looking like it had been carefully placed there by a gigantic hand.

Your Divine Self is continuously taking care of you, and manifesting abundance. Relax, release, and allow your Divine Self to care for you, the terrestrial being.

This earthbound self, along with your consciousness, can go about the business of doing your work. Every day, every moment, revel in your experience of peace, joy, and happiness here and now!

Points for contemplation and action:

- I am the prism through which the laser pure light of abundance breaks out into its potential and is sent forward to provide a light of many colors for others.

- I keep myself creating and at cause. The effects I desire are the result.

- I allow my Divine Self to care for me while I go about my business.

> *"You pray in your distress*
> *and in your need;*
> *would that you might also pray*
> *in the fullness of your joy*
> *and in your days of abundance."*
> ***Kahlil Gibran***

Chapter Eight

Your Source Cares For You

Your Divine Source, living in you, makes all things new and provides you the time to manifest all you are meant to manifest, that you've not yet accomplished.

A natural outcome of that process is, as mentioned, prosperity. Every event, thought, creation, interaction and experience—all issue from Divine Mind, flowing through everything including yourself.

Being awake and attentive clarifies and augments your awareness, your understanding of life, the creative process, Divine Spirit, and the omnipotent Creator.

You would not have come into existence without a plan. You have a purpose.

Be aware of the spirit within you as an unlimited source that fulfills all your needs.

*Your awareness is revealed in everything
you see and do
and in everything that happens to you*

The creator within you is your own cornucopia. It provides your supply of time, creativity, focus, and intention. All you need do is produce clear pictures of your goals and desires. The clearer your mental pictures, the more quickly they are produced.

You can see this with people who have disciplined themselves to picture—imagine or *"image"*—clearly. For example Jack Canfield, Deepak Chopra, Rhonda Byrne, Tony Robbins, and many other great thinkers, creators, writers, and artists, refer, one way and another, to their process of very clearly picturing the outcome of an intention, in order for it to manifest.

Your understanding of your essential internal Spirit, as well as Spirit external to you, significantly contributes to your fullness of life.

Once Again! Prosperity is Not Money

Prosperity is behaviors, things, events, unconditional love, and the light, the *namaste* between you and everyone you meet.

A pile of money is just stuff. It could just as well be a pile of rocks or twigs. But we've agreed that it has a representational quality.
Money is not at cause, and having it or not having it is not at cause.

Money is an *effect*.

It shows you your relationship with being at cause. If you're struggling with money, it has something to do with *your relationship with cause*.

True prosperity is when we bring our awareness of our lovely dream called *LIFE* into balance. It's about understanding the *power of cause*, and the inevitable result in *effect*.

And, further, to create the most perfect, enjoyable, delightful and plentiful experience of life, full to the edges of your imagination and spilling out, like any rich and plentiful cornucopia!

The Essence of the Creator Lives within You— With this Power, You Create

You can make all things new! Energy is continually jockeying and jostling about you. Energy comes through you, as long as you don't block it or interfere with it. Just continue doing what you are called to do. These "doings" come from the well of your being. Prosperity and clarity are born.

Every experience you have is a demonstration—an effect—of your heart's desire. Keep your priorities in order.

Points for contemplation and action:

• Because I exist, there is a plan and a purpose to my life.

• Although prosperity may be in the form of money, it is not money.

• Divine Mind asks me to bring my life into balance.

• I keep my Heart-Mind clear in order to bring through the purest manifestations, which is beneficial for myself, and for all living things.

• The Creator living within me is at cause in my ability to create.

> *"To live a pure unselfish life,
> one must count nothing as one's own
> in the midst of abundance."*
> **Buddha**

Ask your Angels

To make their presence known

Prepare to be amazed

Image & Text © Blythe Ayne

Chapter Nine

Becoming Fulfilled

When you become aware of the power of your Creative Energy, you'll learn that you don't need anything else to become fulfilled.

This is where happiness, joy, and peace, are to be found—right there, at the center of your being. All that you do comes from your Being.

Be Easy with Your Being

Be comfortable in your skin. Like yourself, love yourself, feel natural in what you choose to do. Be easy with your Being.

Effects are in alignment with peace when *cause* is in alignment with peace.

Release worry. Worry is a negative picture/anticipation of the future, which creates a negative future. Why not have a positive anticipation of the future? Worry is a distraction from doing, and a detractor from accomplishment. In short, worry serves no worthwhile function.

You are only in this moment and cannot be in the future. Therefore, worry is a complete waste of energy, as is its "twin emotion," guilt. Guilt is a crippling emotion, hooked up to the past. The past is over and done. Remain in the present, where you have consummate power—if you will only believe it.

Invoke your angels—believe me, they are there!—to assist you in keeping centered and at peace. This is presupposing you have bothered to become acquainted with them. If you haven't, *NOW* would be the perfect time to begin.

Ask your angels to make their presence known, to give you a sign that they are around you. (Prepare to be amazed.)

Divine Mind and Divine Abundance

The Secret of Life is the working of Divine Mind, the center of your Being, combined with Divine Abundance, from which your Doings evolve.

There is no need for further trauma and drama in your life. You've learned those lessons, have you not? Affirm smooth sailing so you can expand and explore your amazing being.

The Creator in You

The facilitator of my meditation group recently took us on a journey through our bodies in meditation. At my crown I experienced tingling, down into my neck, and through my spine, simply *FOCUSING* my attention on these locations.

Further along, at the facilitator's suggestion, my feet went from bitter cold, which they always are! to *HOT* in a few seconds. This demonstrates the power of mind over matter.

Your Creator-Self will obey your directives. You need nothing beyond uncomplicated enjoyment and gratitude, creating a flowing circuit. Plenitude is one charge of the circuit, and gratitude is the other. Creative energy, flowing from gratitude and a belief in plentitude is an unstoppable river, flowing from Divine Consciousness.

The flow comes *through* you, and *is* you.

The Creative Force creates you every day. The Creative Force creates you every, single, moment. And it does so from an infinite well of absolutely unconditional love.

When you are "hooked up," when you are being your true self, you continually flow with creative energy. Your beliefs and actions, that is to say, your work, arise from your being and your doings, mirroring the flow of Divine Prosperity.

Points for contemplation and action:

• Fulfillment comes from my awareness of my Divine Source.

• I will become more aware of my relationship with cause in order to experience different effects.

• I will love myself.

• I release worry—thoughts about the future. It is not here, in the now. Instead, I make positive pictures about the future.

• I release guilt—thoughts about the past. The past is in the past. I bring myself into the present moment, which is the only place I am.

• I will become acquainted with, and closer to, my angels.

> *"Abundance and lack exist simultaneously in our lives, as parallel realities.*
>
> *It is always our conscious choice which secret garden we will tend... when we choose not to focus on what is missing from our lives but are grateful for the abundance that's present...*
>
> *The wasteland of illusion falls away, and we experience Heaven on earth."*
> **Sarah Ban Breathnach**

Chapter Ten

Love—Gratitude—Abundance: Perfect Trinity

Putting it all together:

Keep your focus on the Creator—your *Being*, and the Creative Force—your *Doing*, within you, producing peace and prosperity. This inner presence (cause) is the source of everything that manifests (effects).

Believe in your affluence. *FOCUS* on the God and the Good within you, herein lies your power.

You are a Power Station

Make a picture in your mind of a power station, pulling raw power in, and turning refined power out.

Now make a picture of yourself as this power station.

The light prism at your core—your transformer—takes out all the impurities that come in, and sends the light out crystal clear, transmitting at 100% optimum effectiveness in the form of love, light, joy and peace. Nothing can pass through your purifying crystal without becoming purified, love-filled, and stronger.

A light prism is a vibration of energies. Sound, too, is an energy vibration. Sound creates, Light purifies. Light clears vision, thins the veil, and allows visions. Sound generates the image into three-dimensions.

The inner presence of the fully realized, fully Conscious Being, has control of your prosperity and everything else, such as your creativity, your time, how time passes and what you produce.

Everything, *everything* flows on the river of Love—light, power, gratitude, creation, abundance, the divine and the mundane. Everything from your electric bill to saving the planet floats on the river of Love.

Abundance — Gratitude — Love

Center on the "Abundance—Gratitude—Love" trinity, only giving attention to that which nurtures this energy flux, this energy flow.

Take your attention off the bad mood, the judgmental energy, the compromised self-esteem, which only gum up the smooth workings of the impeccable cogs of abundance and gratitude, components of love.

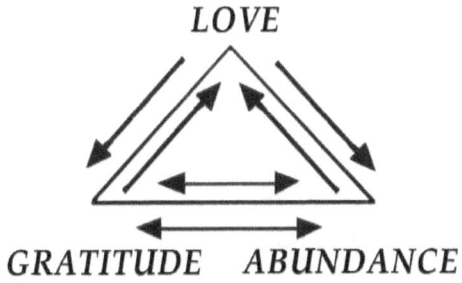

Altogether, this trinity is *the* unstoppable force.

There is limitless generosity in the paradigm of Abundant Creator, Universe, Web of Intelligence, Knowing. You are a node on the web of intelligence. You are capable of augmenting light, knowledge, wisdom, abundance. Send them through you without halting, multiplying into peace, joy, happiness, fulfillment, calm, and dimensional integration.

Remember! Who you are comes from cause. You determine what your cause will set into motion. This is the substance of the visible and the invisible in your life. Understanding this, you will see that more meaningful thoughts, feelings, events, people, and things appear in your life.

Keep your mind off this world in terms of greed and the addiction to "more."

Yes, it's challenging. It's like sitting beside someone with a boom box, woofers turned all the way up so you not only hear the noise, you also feel it.

But you can hear without listening, and therefore, without permitting it to have emotional influence over you. You can acknowledge the noise of greed all around you, without succumbing to it.

Move with Your Intentions

Move in a direction in accordance with your intentions. If it feels blocked, keep moving, affirm that the creator within you has perfect wisdom and will open and shut doors as needed.

You don't need to bang your spiritual head against any of these doors! Your perfect self is continually coming forth from your center, if you let it.

Never lose sight of the fact that you—body, mind, and soul—are an amazing miracle. Your existence is wealth beyond imagining! Be filled with gratitude and love for the great and glorious Gift of Life. Life, itself, is the first experience of the endless outpouring from the Horn of Plenty.

Points for contemplation and action:

- I focus on the light within me, visualizing it crystal clear, a powerful, unconditionally loving, transformer.

- Everything flows on the river of Love. I get in my boat and sing! "Merrily, merrily, merrily, merrily, life is but a dream."

- The creator within me has perfect wisdom.

- This is The Circuit:
  Love = Gratitude = Abundance = Love = Gratitude = Abundance ... to infinity.

> *"If you want love and abundance, give it away."*
> *Anonymous*

The End

Keep your eyes on the light ....

My Gift for You....

Thank you for reading *Horn of Plenty — The Cornucopia of Your Life*. Enter the following web address if you would like to download several posters from *Life Flows on the River of Love*:

http://bit.ly/LifeLifeFlowsonRiverofLove-FreePosters

About the Author ....

I live in a forest with a few domestic and numerous wild creatures, where I create an ever-growing inventory of books, both nonfiction and fiction, short stories, illustrated kid's books, and articles. And I do a bit of wood carving when I need a change of pace.

After I got my Doctorate from the University of California at Irvine in the School of Social Sciences, with a focus on psychology and ethnography, I moved to the Pacific Northwest to write and to have a modest private psychotherapy practice in a small town not much bigger than a village, where I had the privilege of working with amazing people.

But eventually I realized it was time to put my focus on my writing, where, through the world-shrinking internet, I could interact with a greater number of people. Where I could meet you!

Your support of my work contributes to my care of ten acres of natural forest, and all its resident fauna. *All the creatures and I thank you!*

Thoughts, questions, observations? I'd love to hear from you ...

Blythe@BlytheAyne.com

www.BlytheAyne.com

A happy, kind, productive world evolves from happy, kind, productive individual people.

The goal of my writing is to help clear your path to joyful productivity, in the glow of a healthy, contented, and meaningful life.

May All Things
Bright & Beautiful
Fill Your Days
& Dreams of Joy
Fill Your Nights

www.ingramcontent.com/pod-product-compliance
Lightning Source LLC
Chambersburg PA
CBHW030448300426
44112CB00009B/1216